THE PLACE OF THE OLD TESTAMENT IN MODERN RESEARCH

T0345991

CAMBRIDGE
UNIVERSITY PRESS

University Printing House, Cambridge CB2 8BS, United Kingdom

Published in the United States of America by Cambridge University Press, New York

Cambridge University Press is part of the University of Cambridge.

It furthers the University's mission by disseminating knowledge in the pursuit of
education, learning and research at the highest international levels of excellence.

www.cambridge.org
Information on this title: www.cambridge.org/9781107635333

© Cambridge University Press 1932

This publication is in copyright. Subject to statutory exception
and to the provisions of relevant collective licensing agreements,
no reproduction of any part may take place without the written
permission of Cambridge University Press.

First published 1932
Re-issued 2014

A catalogue record for this publication is available from the British Library

ISBN 978-1-107-63533-3 Paperback

Cambridge University Press has no responsibility for the persistence or accuracy of
URLs for external or third-party internet websites referred to in this publication,
and does not guarantee that any content on such websites is, or will remain, accurate
or appropriate.

The
PLACE *of the* OLD TESTAMENT
in MODERN RESEARCH

AN INAUGURAL LECTURE
delivered on 18 May 1932

BY

STANLEY ARTHUR COOK, Litt.D

Regius Professor of Hebrew in the
University of Cambridge

CAMBRIDGE
At the University Press
1932

It was a saying of Scotus Erigena that whatever is true Philosophy is also true Theology. In like manner on a large scale whatever is true History teaches true Religion, and every attempt to reproduce the ages which immediately preceded or which accompanied the advent of Christianity is a contribution, however humble, to the understanding of Christianity itself.

ARTHUR PENRHYN STANLEY
Lectures on the History of the Jewish Church
vol. III, Preface

THE OLD TESTAMENT

IN MODERN RESEARCH

IT is not unnatural that, on an occasion like this, one should think of the men of the past whose labours, whether recognised or not, have combined to bring the study of the Old Testament to its present stage, and the subject which I have chosen for this inaugural lecture will, perhaps, enable us to understand alike our debt to them and the task they have handed on to us.

As I think more especially of the names in this University, and, in particular, of my predecessors in the Chair which it is my high lot to fill for a few years, the name that first arises is that of the late Robert Hatch Kennett. Many of us knew him as one of the kindliest and most stimulating of men, one to whom his pupils—among whom I am proud to have a place—and his colleagues have so recently united in paying spontaneous tribute for all that he meant for them. To follow upon one so gifted as he was is difficult; for he was one whose enthusiasm for his own work he was successful in imparting to others; and all that I can hope is that my own attempt to promote the studies with which this ancient post is associated may show that I am not unmindful of my responsibilities[1].

The history of the development of Oriental studies—in particular of Hebrew and the Old Testament—is a fascinating one. For some four or five centuries they have flourished in unbroken continuity, such that at the present day we find ourselves borne along, as it were, upon a steadily flowing stream which, indeed, cannot be stopped, though, to be sure, we may shape its course. What that course will be one cannot foretell, but it is only as we observe the trend of centuries of research in these studies that we obtain a true insight into the possibilities of their future.

My subject, "The Place of the Old Testament in Modern Research," is necessarily bound up both with the growth of intelligent interest in Oriental and Biblical studies and with the particular aspects, questions, or even controversies, which, at one time or another, have held the stage. The progress of our several studies depends upon our special problems which are felt to be of primary importance, and upon their relation to other problems perhaps of more immediate or practical or popular interest. The particular problems in our field to-day are not those of the past; yet when, for example, the burning question was the antiquity of the Hebrew vowel-points, this was not a merely academic controversy, but was involved in the graver question of verbal inspiration. In like manner, the literary problem of the composition of the Pentateuch and the archaeological problem even of the fall of Jericho are not merely of academic importance or for specialists alone, in that profounder matters, whether they are always visible or not, may be found lurking not far distant.

The question of the Place of the Old Testament in Modern Research turns out to be bound up with the history of thought. To have put the title of this lecture in the form of a question would recall the fact that in Hebrew the rhetorical question is a forcible denial, and that there are, in truth, those who for one reason or another are convinced that the Old Testament no longer has any value for us, or at least for our research. Moreover, there are those, also, who believe that the major problems of the last generation have been settled finally, and that the Old Testament has left little for active minds to pursue. On the other hand, yet others are there who believe that these problems are still far from solution; and sometimes it would almost appear as though certain fundamental questions which are the concern of the Old Testament student and which, one thought, had been settled once and for all, are again cast into the melting-pot. Now it is not my intention to discuss here the rights or wrongs of what is known as the Higher Criticism; there is something more vital than the question whether the views of such and such men are conservative or moderate or advanced, it is the necessity of understanding and of restating the place of Old Testament study in the world of scholarly thought.

I propose, first, to touch very briefly upon the growth of Semitic and Biblical studies in the West, and I may be pardoned if, while not indifferent to the international character of research, I make special reference to this University. I shall then say something on the nature of Old Testament research of the last few decades. From the way in which different lines of study have contributed to our present knowledge of the Old Testament and its field, I shall pass to the way in which the debt is being repaid. It seems to me that our newer knowledge of what, in old-fashioned language, we call the "Bible lands" has much to contribute to the profounder problems which are not the concern of the mere Hebraist or of the student of the Old Testament as such. Here it is that, as I believe, one can show the very real importance of our study, and that if the Bible was once, in a sense, the centre and criterion of all knowledge, it is regaining a position in the world of thought which manifests anew its uniqueness, and its significance for research.

The growth of Hebrew and other Semitic studies in the western world has been traced by competent pens[2]. For many centuries Christians desirous of information on the interpretation of the Old Testament were perforce obliged to consult Jews, some of whom, as we know, were converts. There were a few Christians—of whom the Venerable Bede (about A.D. 700) may have been one —who seem to have possessed a small knowledge of Hebrew; and there were not a few who found a mystical value in the Hebrew script and a certain magical potency in the Hebrew language, and, then as now, it would happen that an untutored and more or less emotional interest in the strange and the curious would sometimes lead to an interest that was more intelligent and fruitful.

One would like to dwell upon the part played by Arabs and Jews in the transmission of learning during the so-called Dark Ages: the School of Baghdad, the different migrations westwards along the shores of the

Mediterranean to Spain and France, the renown of Jewish physicians, the theological and philosophical activity of Semites who directly and indirectly provoked—and not always in the best sense of the word—the scholars of Western Europe. These Orientals had much to contribute to the West, although, even in the thirteenth century, Roger Bacon, himself "a tolerable Hebrew scholar," could lament that among the Latins there were not four who had a grammatical knowledge of Hebrew, or Arabic, or even Greek. However, we are indebted to Dominican and Franciscan missionary zeal for the encouragement of Oriental studies in Europe, and the year 1276 is marked by the first Oriental College, Raymond Lull's, in Mallorca. It was at Miramar, and the visitor to that lovely site will deplore the old-time depressing notion in this country that learning would flourish best in surroundings less conducive to physical well-being.

Those were days when Arabic and Hebrew were being studied by men whose lives were devoted to converting Saracen and Jew. But to confute the Semite and to proselytise were not their only aims. There were men interested in going behind the corrupt text of the Latin Vulgate; and while Philosophy, Astronomy and Astrology, Mathematics and Medicine turned some to Arabic and Hebrew learning, others, men of Neo-Platonic sympathies, were fascinated by the Jewish mystical Kabbalah, or, in reaction against an arid scholasticism, found new and more refreshing treasures in the religious literature of the Jews. The part played by this medieval Jewish mysticism in the history of Hebrew studies is a curious little chapter in itself.

But it was not until the sixteenth century that Oriental research was definitely started on its course, and this University begins to take a leading part. Passing over John Fisher's lectureships in Greek and Hebrew (1501), we note first the famous school of theology at Louvain, the Collegium Trilingue, exclusively devoted to the study of Latin, Greek and Hebrew. It was visited by men from Cambridge, and notably by Robert Wakefield. Hebrew professor at Louvain

(1515), he succeeded in establishing a reputation successively at Tübingen, Cambridge (1524) and Christ Church, Oxford (1530), and was reputed the first linguist of his time.

Those were days of practical enthusiasm for the new learning, and whereas a couple of centuries earlier we read, for example, that the Abbot of Westminster in 1325 sent to Oxford a contribution of $17\frac{1}{2}d$. "for the expenses of the masters lecturing in the Hebrew, Arabic and Chaldean languages at the University," now, on two occasions when Cambridge was suffering from serious financial stringency, the University lecturer in mathematics was suspended in order that his stipend might go to the lecturers in Hebrew and Greek[3].

When, in 1540, the Regius Professorships were established here—the first instalment of the funds from the dissolution of the monasteries—an immediate impetus was given to the study of Greek and Latin. But the Hebrew professor, Thomas Wakefield, a younger brother of the more famous Robert, suffered through the religious controversies

of the age, his tenure of office was inter-
mittent, and a series of foreigners, Jews, in-
cluding the famous Fagius and Tremellius,
leave their mark upon Hebrew studies [4].
Even in the seventeenth century we have to
look, for the best work, outside the Hebrew
Professors, and Ralph Cudworth, the great
leader of the Cambridge Platonists, has scarcely
any Hebrew reputation save as regards the
composition of such odes as then and later
were expected of the occupants of the Chair [5].

Yet splendid work was done in that century.
It must suffice to refer, quite summarily, to
the Authorised Version, and the great Arab-
ists: William Bedwell of Cambridge with his
renowned Oxford pupil Edward Pococke,
and Abraham Wheelock, the first Arabic Professor, and his famous pupil Thomas Hyde,
later of Oxford. John Selden of Oxford
opened out a new world by his researches
in Semitic Mythology (1617), and John
Spencer, Master of Corpus Christi College,
Cambridge, has not unjustly been styled the
founder of Comparative Religion. Rabbinic
studies flourished, through the remarkable

14

learning and energy of John Lightfoot, greatest of Christian Rabbinical scholars, and the Mishnah was first translated here by the Jew, Isaac Abendana, no doubt through his stimulus [6].

But above all must mention be made of the band of men who produced Brian Walton's great Polyglot Bible: a gigantic task, considering the age—and also a commercial success. We of to-day can have nothing but admiration for Castell, Thorndyke and the other scholars, some traces of whose work are preserved in our University Library. It is of peculiar interest that, as Mullinger tells us, although the Polyglot was produced in an age of the bitterest political and ecclesiastical strife, men rose above controversy; and the fierce differences of the Cromwellian period did not prevent the preparation and publication of a work of incalculable value, a European event, which, perhaps, gave birth to that phrase, current in the seventeenth century, *Clerus Anglicanus stupor Mundi* [7].

Were it possible to give here a less scanty

outline of these studies, we should be struck by the ebb and flow in their history. We should recognise what we owe to Popes and Cardinals, to Dominicans and Franciscans. Then we should turn to the zeal of the Reformers for the original languages of the Bible; and we should find that Greek was feared by their opponents because it was the road to heresy, the study of Hebrew and Greek being the occupation of heretics[8]. Having discharged our debt to the Reformation, we should encounter the Puritan dislike of strange tongues, of Latin, Greek and Hebrew[9]. At one time there would be absurd and false estimates of the value of Hebrew, and at another men would be lamenting its decay.

In brief, a survey of the course of these studies would show us our indebtedness varyingly to Christians and to Jews, to Roman Catholics and to Protestants, to bitter controversy and to friendly co-operation (e.g. of Christians and Jews). There would be alternatively periods of decline and of new energy—both often entirely explicable—and an extraordinary variety of motives in the progressive development of Hebrew and Old Testament knowledge. It is true that after the seventeenth century we seem to have a period of stagnation, a Dark Age as it were, but it is only a partial eclipse; and when we come to the nineteenth century we discover that the road has meanwhile been silently laid for the remarkable and somewhat spectacular progress which the last 80 or 100 years have witnessed.

Before I turn to these I should like to refer, in passing, to the philosophical importance of the comparative study of the *history* of different studies. The periods of stagnation, the "Dark Ages" in a study, are not—regarded philosophically—very different from those in the actual history of a people or land. There are such "Dark Ages" in Egypt, Babylonia and Assyria, and elsewhere; but we know enough to say that they are only relatively dark, and that when we regard the drama of their history from an evolutionary point of view, the curtain is merely being lowered and the stage set for the next period of active progress. There are problems of the Old Testament which turn upon the fact that the processes in history—whether lands, peoples or fields of research—have the same sort of complexity; and it is not going too far to say that the most fundamental questions in the interpretation of the Old Testament, questions of the evolution or development of the beliefs and customs of Israel, would be clearer if we understood more clearly the typical processes in the history of some field of thought, such as Biblical research itself.

Characteristic of modern Biblical research is its emancipation from earlier associations. Oriental studies have freed themselves from Oriental tutelage, the interpreters of the Old Testament go behind Jewish exegetes and the Bible is approached in the light of new rather than of old knowlege. Indeed, Western rather than Eastern thought has enlarged our general knowledge of the Book, and other than Jewish minds have advanced the interpretation of the Old Testament. But whether that is entirely an advantage, and whether it will always be so, is another matter.

The present position of Old Testament research is due to a variety of causes which may be conveniently arranged under five heads.

First, the great steps taken in linguistic study. Here, besides our vastly superior knowledge of long known languages such as Hebrew, Arabic and Chaldee (or Aramaic as it is now called), must be counted the discovery and decipherment of various long-forgotten languages, notably, of course, Egyptian and Akkadian (i.e. Babylonian and Assyrian), and, more recently, Hittite.

Second, the internal study of the Old Testament, its text and the problems arising therefrom (their literary origin, historical value, etc., etc.). The history of this study is a subject in itself, and we may recall in passing how a former Regius Professor of Hebrew, H. Lloyd, towards the close of the eighteenth century, tried in vain to obtain ecclesiastical and university permission for a translation of Eichhorn's once influential but now antiquated *Introduction to the Old Testament*, a book that is an important landmark in the history of Biblical Criticism[10].

Third, an immense amount of "external" material has been accumulated, partly in the shape of the more or less contemporary evidence of ancient monuments, tablets and papyri, and partly, the purely archaeological evidence of excavation and of inscribed objects, material which almost invariably stands in need of interpretation or explanation.

Fourth, the comparative study of beliefs and customs, which we especially associate with the names of Robertson Smith and Sir James Frazer, has thrown a flood of light upon the Old Testament, and has brought the people of Israel out of that isolation in which they had seemed to live.

Finally, the study of the Old Testament in the light of all this "external" evidence has so illumined the background and environment of the Bible as a whole, that not only has Biblical research been completely revolutionised in the course of the last generation or so, but it is difficult, even for the expert or specialist, to grasp and estimate all that is being done in his field.

We are confronted with the fact that the

amount of material has outrun methods of dealing with it. Renan once said of the Arabic Lexicon that with a little good-will one could get out of a text any meaning one wanted; and, certainly, as regards the Old Testament, it is unfortunately possible by appropriate reference to this or the other dictionary, or to this or the other belief or custom, and especially by the promiscuous combination of the most widely diverse material, to proffer explanations and theories which sometimes do not even deserve the compliment of being called improbable or impossible. Such is the medley of literature called forth by the masses of material directly or indirectly bearing upon the Old Testament that the problem of organising the material must be solved, in the interests of the progressive development of the study of the Bible. The solution will be suggested later (p. 37).

The Old Testament is a Sacred Book, bound up with non-religious lines of research. The folk-lorist, the archaeologist, the psychologist and the psycho-analyst, and the student of secular history—each in turn utilises the Book, and each in his own way contributes to our knowledge of it. If, then, we are struck by the absence of uniformity in the way it is treated, the cause lies, partly, in the absence of uniformity in these other studies, whether we regard them as ancillary or as independent. To put it otherwise, the Old Testament cannot be held apart as a religious book, nor can it be ignored on that or any other ground. Whatever may be thought of the way in which it should be taught in schools, when the intelligent child enters the large world outside, the Old Testament is constantly brought before him, directly or indirectly—the tomb of Tut-ankh-amen, the walls of Jericho, Hatshepsut, the alleged patronness of Moses—and he is ill-prepared to face the conflicting and confusing opinions in the literature accessible to him. Indeed, the progress of research, discoveries in the "Bible-Lands" and the growth of Comparative Religion are more than likely to bring to the fore the problem of the Sacred Book and the people.

Between the specialist and that useful fig-
ment "the man in the street" are the many
mediating and compromising ventures with
which we are all familiar. I myself should
be the last to decry them, for they are indispensable; but it must be said that often
they are more spectacular than sound, and
give an entirely misleading picture of the
state of our Biblical knowledge. I should be
the last to belittle what we owe to Archaeology and the Monuments—I owe so much
to a subject in which I have always been
keenly interested—but it is unfortunately the
archaeologist who, from time to time, well-
meaning, though with unjustifiable assurance,
goes beyond his evidence and gives a false
impression of what Archaeology really is
doing for our study. And it must be ad-
mitted that the fault lies less with the archaeologist than with the student of the Bible and
is due to the incomplete methodology of our
special field of research.

The Old Testament is an integral part of
Ancient History—*that* was first shown con-
clusively by Joseph Scaliger nearly four cen-

turies ago—its religion is an integral part of the history of the World's Religion—here John Spencer, nearly three centuries ago, is a landmark. What this means has hardly yet been realised. We know only that we cannot pursue our studies in isolation, and that the general principles and methods in our field cannot be wholly severed from those in other fields. But each is able to contribute to the other, for it is by the natural convergence of results and by co-operation, rather than by mechanical borrowing, or by the arbitrary subordination of one branch of learning to another, that the progressive development of thought has hitherto been due.

So, it will now be understood that questions of popular interest, whether the fall of the walls of Jericho, or the monotheistic religion before Moses, are of little abiding importance for us, partly because they are handled in a way that is singularly unhelpful —though one hesitates to interfere, seeing that all of us are aiming at the same goal—and partly also because there are problems of history and religion of much greater and more permanent significance. The place of the Old Testament in world-history and world-religion is unique, and we are obtaining a new and vastly clearer conception of all that wherein the uniqueness lies. Hence, although it is true to say that there are Old Testament scholars who doubt this piece of evidence, or deny the other, the fuller knowledge which we are gaining of history and religion is more inspiring for us, and especially for this very age, than what was known when, four or five centuries ago, the study of the Bible began to be inaugurated and the doctrine of Literal Inspiration held the field.

Earlier notions of Universal History were necessarily subordinated to the Old Testament account of Creation and the Dispersion of Man after the Flood. But these have been or, rather, are in course of being replaced by one in which the Old Testament has a very different though still unique place. To-day we can pass from astrophysics and physics to the dawn of life; we can leave behind us pre-history and proto-history, and, entering upon the relatively brief story of civilisation—the difficult art of learning to live together—we can endeavour to trace the steps in the growth of man's knowledge of the Universe and of its God, a God who is his own.

Thus, new knowledge of the past is slowly being built up. Already there are massive works which few can digest; and there are the smaller and more popular works which usually do scant justice to the historical and religious value of the Old Testament. Some day a great Epic of Man will be written, but only after the material has been tested, assimilated and co-ordinated. In the meantime, much can be done, not only in furthering our present knowledge, but also in reconsidering those matters that influence our attitudes to facts, and in revising the regulative principles we unconsciously employ when we handle them.

Here I should like to refer in particular to two questions where a better knowledge of the past is full of meaning for the present. As we look back upon past history—a past of which the Bible is an organic part—we are struck by the interdependence of peoples, and by special periods of exceptional creative power. We trace back our culture to Rome and Greece, and to the Near East, and recognise the world's debt to the great monotheisms of the Lands of the Bible. But we find, from prehistoric times onwards, a certain amount of migration, trade-intercourse, the periodic spread of definite influences and, in general, an inter-relationship occasionally amounting to what without exaggeration we may call internationalism. At certain times non-Semitic influence was exceptionally strong; and while the Persian rule over Palestine in the days of post-exilic Israel had its forerunner round about the Mosaic age, when Indo-Iranian elements left their mark upon that land, many centuries later, when the Semites kept alive the torch of learning in the early Middle Ages, it was specially the non-Semitic Mohammedan—a Persian it might be—to whom much is due. Incalculable and unforgettable though our debt is to Jews and Arabs, it is more than questionable whether we do not owe most to the clash of minds of different racial origin. Even as regards the Old Testament itself, there is a sense in which its permanent value for religion can be ascribed to other than Hebraic or Israelite or Jewish factors alone[11].

The Comparative Study of Religions traces remarkable parallels between Biblical, Semitic and other ideas and practices, and it is only when we seem to have deprived the Old Testament of all that once was thought to be peculiar to it that we discover how much more brightly its distinctiveness shines forth. The more the religion and history of Palestine appear to be submerged in the religion and history of its environment, the more impressive is all that which makes the Old Testament unique, and which causes us, in our retrospect, to look back there and not elsewhere. It is the specific forms of certain more or less universal beliefs and ideas which have been so effective: the particular ideas of God, Man and the Universe, ideas often similar to, yet in some sense—which requires to be reformulated—different from and more effective than those in other lands.

Let me say, in passing, that if we hail this

result, it is well to bear in mind the cost at which it has been reached—the errors, extravagances and failures which litter the path of this as of every other piece of successful research, and for which we must always be prepared if we wish to maintain our freedom. Moreover, it is often forgotten that when we accept such significant results on the authority of others, they are not uncommonly part of a larger complex which we are not at liberty to accept or reject at pleasure. So, as regards the "criticism" of the Old Testament, there is a widespread acceptance of some general results—indeed, among archaeologists there is a very noteworthy acceptance of certain vital theories—but it is necessary to observe that various typical objections and protests will proceed from the mouths of those who have not realised the inevitable implications of that to which they have already assented. The acceptance of the rights of Biblical Criticism is far more sweeping and fundamental than the rejection—on whatever grounds—of any particular "critical" conclusion.

To return. We desire to understand more clearly what it is that has been so effective in the line of progressive development upon which we can look back. And as we ponder over what is due to the religious and historical development which we can trace in Palestine, we feel that the price we have to pay for our deeper insight into the processes of the past is the task of contributing to their further advance. It is difficult to resist the conviction that the history of the past is most truly interpreted when our retrospect has some meaning for the future.

As we look back, certain periods stand out apart from others. Not only the First Century of the Christian Era, some centuries earlier another great period can be recognised in the history of Israel. And there are also others to which it is unnecessary to refer now. These are periods which in certain essential respects resemble one another, and of such periods the present also seems to be one. There are many technical problems of the Old Testament, or rather of the Bible as a whole, which turn upon the sort of changes that occur in such periods, and the deeper study of the past is thus by no means of merely academic importance. The real nature of that development which we trace back to the Ancient Near East and the inwardness of certain outstanding periods—and here that of the Renaissance and the Reformation will not be overlooked—do more than excite our curiosity; we feel that here are problems, the solution of which—nay, rather, the very effort to solve which—will teach us much more of ourselves and our Universe.

As we look back over the past we observe the inseparable interconnections of thought between the Old Testament and the New. The student of the New Testament may be content with a minimum of the Old Testament, but the student of the Old Testament finds himself carried forward into the New—if not to nearer ages. Elsewhere, in Egypt, Babylonia, India and China, we can trace continuity and even development, but there is not that pregnancy, we miss that progressive development which seems to be capable of new growth the more clearly we understand its past stages.

Monotheism or monotheistic tendencies can be traced outside Israel, but only the ethical monotheism of Israel was effective; and neither the sublime ideas we find elsewhere, nor so lofty a conception of Deity as that of the old Indian god Varuna, bore fruit[12]. Jews spread the ethical doctrine of their God, and in course of time Christianity was carried to the East as well as to the West; but we are justified in pointing to that particular line of progressive development which connects us here and now with a far-off ancestry, and in regarding it as a summons to understand our place in the curve of history.

Bernhard Duhm, one of the finest of Old Testament commentators, has observed that to say "God made history," is of more value than to say "God made the world." What Lord Acton, in his inaugural lecture on "The Study of History," said, both in his lecture and in his invaluable collection of notes, touching Providence and History, needs no retelling; but though we are at one with Duhm in seeing a divine process throughout all history, it is a task and a privilege, each according to his ability, to learn what can be learnt from that interplay of events that has brought mankind to its present position.

It is not without significance that a sense of history—the feeling of belonging to a process that is still working among us, a process incarnate in men—has played a vital part both in the pregnant events that lie behind the Old Testament—and the New—and in the more recent efforts to recover and understand the past. But although some theory of evolution, that is, an evolutionary way of looking at things, is found to be indispensable— at least, if the Old Testament is to be intelligently understood—the best sort of theory has not yet been found. Thus, certain evolutionary reconstructions of the religious and social development of Israel are no longer tenable; the problem proves to be much more complex than one had thought, and the simple, straightforward outlines, which are familiar to us in our books, tend to be more misleading than helpful.

This statement which I have made must not be misunderstood. To construct an intelligible outline of Old Testament history and religion, every writer, whatever his standpoint, must ignore much evidence that conflicts with or contradicts the data upon which he relies. This is due to the composite character of the contents of the Old Testament, the ages over which they range, and the diverse circles amid which they rose or through which they passed. Now our aim is to find a reconstruction which does justice to *all* the data that are crying for recognition. The task is thereby aggravated, but we are impelled by the faith that we *must* find a standpoint from which we can take in a larger mass of material than we do at present.

Whatever historical reconstruction—and it will have to be of an evolutionary character —comes to hold the field, meanwhile certain impressive facts deserve notice. We cannot look upon Old Testament history as a single coherent unit, *uno tenore*. On the contrary, when the Old Testament is viewed historically we see ebb and flow, growth and decay, enthusiasm and pessimism, faith and despair[13]. Prophets differing widely in spiritual

34

calibre, priest-prophets and priests have each their day. Now the keynote is individualism, and now the claims of the social group as a whole. At one time, a people of priests, every man the prophet of the Lord; at another, organisation and select representatives. Or a new age is longed for, anticipated; and when the new age has been inaugurated, it has not brought what men hoped: *plus ça change*.... Such vicissitudes lie behind the progressive development that can be traced in the Old Testament; and the Old Testament is not a Book from which to select proof-texts at will, but has behind it a drama which, as we begin to understand and realise it, has a purifying effect upon us who live in an age of dramatic history. It was the recognition that the Bible was a living force in history, and not—to use Luther's words—"a bag of oats" to grub in unintelligently[14], which marked the new stage in thought, some four centuries ago, when Hebrew studies entered definitely upon their new career; and it is once more a new way of looking at the Bible which we are gradually acquiring, thanks to the interdependence of the various branches of modern research.

So, if the Old Testament is fascinating from the purely historical point-of-view, it is also sobering; for we, too, may hope for and work for a millennium, some new age, but there will be subsequent disappointments, and reactions, and no generation can lay down the tracks along which the next shall run. Yet in the history of the past, just as in the history of research itself, each stage is the heir of its predecessors, and its diverse and often conflicting elements are introducing the next stage. But at each stage there are specific tendencies, special needs, when one problem or group of problems will stand out above the rest and more clamantly demand attention. The course of history—whether in the Old Testament, or in research itself—would seem to be determined by the conscious or unconscious recognition of that pre-eminent task to which are subordinated all other tasks; and these are sometimes found to become of really minor importance or will take another aspect.

It is thus that the problem of organising our material may be settled (see p. 21).

At the present day we are recognising the philosophical importance of the field of history as a whole, and the philosophy of the future will be based upon a vastly larger induction of facts of history and religion than were available to the great founders and leaders of the past. But it is not as clearly recognised, perhaps, not only that there is a philosophy as well as a psychology of research, but that the attempt of the "arm-chair students" to do justice to large masses of data is not wholly diverse from the practical attempt of the men of affairs to do justice to the masses of not less vociferous material in the world at large.

But I must pass on and come to the point. The urgent task in the field of Old Testament study is to find a standpoint such that the innumerable problems, great and small, will fall into position, and that the special problem which we consider to be of the first importance shall direct our studies and shape the rest. Such a pre-eminent problem is surely that of the great creative periods in history, periods of disintegration and redintegration, of decay and fresh growth. Both the Old Testament and the New turn upon such periods, and the many questions which they involve both illumine and are illumined by the age in which we live. It remains to offer some remarks by way of justification.

The period to which belongs the Exile of Israel, the sixth century B.C., was one of an outburst of activity not confined to the Near East. Why is it that then, and not then alone, there is a certain simultaneity that has impressed independent historians?[15] At present we can hardly venture an answer. In Israel alone is there a progressive development; and from the Old Testament we can endeavour to determine the factors. Here the part played by the prophets has always appealed to us, though not for the same reason; and it is no exaggeration to say that from time to time we are finding something new in their utterances or in their personality. We cannot understand them unless we can understand the "false" prophets, and we perceive that the essence of "true" prophetism seems to lie, not in foretelling or anticipating the future, but in helping men to face *any* future and in paving the way for the establishment of those essential principles upon which depends man's fullest happiness in the Universe. Not the pressure of the environment upon man, but man's power to cope with and to shape it is what the "true" prophets have to tell. When the best of them are headed by Amos, the prophet of divine righteousness, and Hosea, the prophet of divine love, we think of Browning's words, "all's love yet all's law"; and we marvel at those processes of development or evolution whereby this complementary pair stand at the head. Indeed, if, as is sometimes contended, these and other prophets were ecstatics, we may be pardoned if we regret that their affliction was not contagious!

The study of such figures contributes to psychology, and much has been written from a more or less psychological standpoint concerning prophets, mystics, and the like. It is the *content* of their experiences which now

39

calls for closer attention. But whereas we are familiar with the significance of those experiences for our ideas of ultimate reality, we cannot overlook the not less significant fact, enshrined in the Book of Micah, that, from the point of view of Divine Reality, special ceremonial, ritual and psychical conditions are not so essential as simple justice and righteous doing. Little wonder that for our enquiries into the profounder problems of existence we find in what, following Robertson Smith, we may call the Old Testament "theories" of religion, a starting-point for some new and more comprehensive "theory" of reality[16].

We would probe more deeply into the circumstances of that insight of the old seers. The appreciation of their worth and the critical study of the Old Testament have moved, and will, I believe, continue to move together; and there are numerous technical questions in a field which requires enthusiastic and trained workers, and not Hebraists alone. The work before us is arduous and delicate, but there is a new world to be opened out. Let me give an illustration of the present incompleteness of one aspect of the task.

We value the Old Testament for its spiritual worth, but it reflects conditions against which prophets and priests in turn contended. We cannot have any blind enthusiasm for the ancient Hebrews or the Semites—no one could have been more bitter opponents than the great reforming and constructive figures through whose work our Old Testament is what it is and has permanent worth. Nothing would be gained by quoting the utterly candid, uncompromising, forceful estimates of the ancient Semites by men like Robertson Smith, Doughty, Lawrence, Kennett, Nöldeke and others[17]. There, as in war-time, we see the heights and depths of men. We are tempted to concentrate solely upon the one or upon the other, though as students—and not merely as students—we have to see things steadily and as a whole, and hope to become kinder and wiser in our judgements. We have to reach an attitude to enable us to deal fairly with our material. It is an ordeal, and a discipline, but one gains a truer view of humanity, and thereby have ourselves made some advance. In both history and research an advance is made by reaching a new attitude to the "material" that perplexes and distresses us.

So far as we can understand the great creative period in Israel, the disasters of the Exilic period that might have brought pessimism and death brought new hope, the very evil led to the new realisation of good, the disintegration and discontinuity gave birth to new ideas of fresh growth and continuity; and the age which saw the decline and decay of great surrounding powers "happens" also to be the age of the high-water mark in the religious development of Israel. "Happens," I say, but behind these generalising remarks lie great questions clamouring for attention.

In the course of research, as in the history of a people, there are periods of confusion when it is difficult to sever true from false, and the pregnant from the sterile; yet just as one may see the dawn of a new tendency in one's own field of research, the belief may be cherished that the endeavour to understand to the uttermost those tremendous movements which have ultimately brought us to where we now are will give us a profoundly grander conception of the part we may be called upon to play.

To conclude. The Old Testament has an organic place in modern research by reason both of the many diverse studies that contribute to our knowledge of it, and of the unique contribution that it, in its turn, makes to a deeper knowledge of ourselves. By reason of its position in the great field of History and Religion we must expect that, as the work of criticism becomes more penetrating, the results will be very differently estimated; but to me, at least, it is clear that the gains will continue, as always, immeasurably to outweigh what, for the time being, may be felt to be losses. Moreover, at certain epochs new positive additions are made to Thought, and it seems to me that the explicit and definitive recognition of the natural place of the Old Testament—the

Bible—in the commonwealth of studies which are collectively for the advancement of Man, will, once and for all, correct any timid obscurantism and remove the possibility of a relapse into the bygone thought of a bygone period of history.

No doubt one may be tempted to believe that, on a variety of grounds, one's own country has here a characteristic contribution of its own to make to the future. But one remembers that in Assyria, in the seventh century B.C., the accumulation of material was followed immediately by the sudden, amazing decline of its empire; and that while the student of the history of Palestine is struck by the progressive development of life and thought in Israel round about the seventh to fifth centuries B.C.—the enquiry into which is *the* fundamental problem of the Old Testament—only a few centuries pass and it proved impossible for Palestine to make a further advance, and the line of history takes an entirely different course which could never have been foreseen.

Our Old Testament and Hebrew studies

to-day find their most definite starting-point, some four centuries or so ago, in the days of the New Learning, when men were perplexed and distressed at the disappearance of old beacons, and were uncertain of the direction along which they seemed to be drifting. Those were also the days when men had sailed westwards to discover new shores, and a new route to the East. In each case Faith has been justified of her children. Our position to-day has grown so naturally and unconsciously out of the humble faith and quiet courage of past generations and their desire to search out the deep things of Providence, that we ourselves are urged to look forward to new shores rather than to return to the safety of the havens whence we—or they—started. Indeed, though it is sometimes suggested that we who devote ourselves to Biblical subjects are "at sea," are there not among us those who believe that already there are signs that these new shores are not far distant? And if I may pursue this train of thought, I would add that the direction along which we are being borne is not a new approach to an old world, but to new realms in the domain of Thought awaiting peaceful conquest, in friendly rivalry for a common end.

NOTES

[1] I may be permitted to refer to my appreciation of Kennett's work in the current *Journal of Theological Studies*.

[2] I have drawn upon the chapters by Dr Charles Singer and Dr G. H. Box in *The Legacy of Israel* (ed. by E. Bevan and Singer, 1927); J. B. Mullinger, *The University of Cambridge*, 3 vols. (see Index *s.v.* Hebrew); and Gottheil's article, "Hebraists (Christian)," in the *Jewish Encyclopaedia*. The Reader in Rabbinics (Mr Herbert Loewe) has also drawn my attention to articles in the *Transactions* of the Jewish Historical Society, vii. 1–19 (S. A. Hirsch), viii. 1 *sqq.*; "The Hebrew Treasures of England" (Elkan Adler); *ibid*. 63 *sqq.*, 78 *sqq.*, 98 *sqq.* (Israel Abrahams, C. E. Sayle, and H. P. Stokes), ix. 10 *sqq.* and x. 221 *sqq.* (Abrahams).

[3] See *Legacy of Israel*, p. 306; Mullinger ii (1884), 51 and n. 2 (the two occasions were 1535 and 1537).

[4] J. R. Tanner, *Historical Register of the University of Cambridge* (1917), p. 76; *Legacy of Israel*, p. 334.

[5] See Abrahams, *Transactions* of the Jew. Hist. Soc., ix. 103 *sqq.*

[6] *Ibid*. viii. 98 *sqq.*

7 Quoted by Dr G. H. Box, *Legacy of Israel*, p. 368.

8 Cf. *Legacy*, p. 319; Mullinger, i. 486.

9 Mullinger, iii. 388 *sq.*

10 T. K. Cheyne, *Founders of Old Testament Criticism* (1893), pp. 22, 195.

11 See *Journal of Theological Studies*, xxxii (1931), 240 *sqq.*

12 *Ibid.* xxxiii (1931), 6 *sq.*

13 *Ibid.* xxx (1929), 302 *sqq.*; xxvi. 171 *sqq.*; xxix. 17 *sq.*

14 Quoted from *Lectures and Essays of W. Robertson Smith*, p. 210.

15 *The Cambridge Ancient History*, iv. 118; cf. p. 538 (for the prelude, see *ibid.* iii., Synchronistic Table, No. ii, under 720 B.C.). See further, Dean Stanley, *The Jewish Church*, ii (1876), p. xvi *sq.*; G. F. Moore, *History of Religions*, i, p. 8 *sq.*, and for earlier periods, Ed. Meyer, *Gesch. d. Altertums*, i, §§ 592 *sqq.*; also the present writer's article in the *Encyc. Britannica* (14th ed.) xiii. 26, col. 2.

16 See *The Old Testament in the Jewish Church* (2nd Ed., 1892), pp. 285, 291, 306; and the present writer's *Ethical Monotheism in the Light of Comparative Religion* (a lecture before the West London Synagogue Association, 34 Upper Berkeley Street, London, W. 1, by whom it is published).

17 *Lectures and Essays of W. Robertson Smith*, p. 425; Nöldeke (see A. A. Bevan, in *Journal of the Royal Asiatic Society*, April, 1931, p. 495 *sq.*); E. Lawrence (Preface to Doughty's *Arabia Deserta*, i, p. xxx *sq.*); Kennett (see S. A. Cook, in *Journ. of Theol. Studies*, xxxiii (1932), p. 228); and cf. *Camb. Anc. Hist.* i. 196 *sqq.*, 200 *sq.*

www.ingramcontent.com/pod-product-compliance
Ingram Content Group UK Ltd.
Pitfield, Milton Keynes, MK11 3LW, UK
UKHW020448010325
455719UK00015B/480

9 781107 635333